IS-0100.c: An Introduction to the Incident Command System, ICS 100

Student Manual
Date Released: 11/2018

Published by Michigan Legal Publishing Ltd.
Grand Rapids, Michigan

Academic and bulk discounts available at
www.michlp.com

ISBN: 978-1-64002-087-0

Contents

Lesson 1: Course Welcome and ICS Overview

Visual 1:   Course Welcome

This course will introduce students to the Incident Command System (ICS). This system is used nationwide to manage incidents regardless of size or type.

This is the first in a series of ICS courses for all personnel involved in incident management. Descriptions and details about the other ICS courses in the series may be found on our web site: http://training.fema.gov.

Visual 2:   <u>Course Goal</u>

The overall course goal is to promote effective response by:

- Familiarizing you with the Incident Command System (ICS) and the NIMS principles used to manage incidents.
- Preparing you to coordinate with response partners from all levels of government and the private sector.

IS-100.c provides information on ICS which is part of the National Incident Management System (NIMS). To learn more about NIMS following completion of this course, you can take IS-700.b: An Introduction to the National Incident Management System.

Visual 3:   <u>Overall Course Objectives</u>

At the completion of this course, you should be able to:

- Explain the principles and basic structure of the Incident Command System (ICS).
- Describe the NIMS management characteristics that are the foundation of the ICS.
- Describe the ICS functional areas and the roles of the Incident Commander and Command Staff.
- Describe the General Staff roles within ICS.
- Identify how NIMS management characteristics apply to ICS for a variety of roles and discipline areas.

Visual 4:   <u>Student Introductions</u>

Introduce yourself by providing:

- Your name
- Your job title
- A brief statement of your overall experience with emergency or incident response
- Your possible roles in responding to incidents

Visual 5:   <u>Student Expectations</u>

?

What do you expect to gain from this course?

Visual 6:   <u>Course Structure</u>

The course is divided into the following five units:
- Unit 1: Course Welcome and ICS Overview
- Unit 2: NIMS Management Characteristics
- Unit 3: ICS Functional Areas and Command Staff Roles
- Unit 4: General Staff Roles
- Unit 5: How ICS Applies to You

Visual 7:   <u>Course Logistics</u>

Review the following information:

- Course agenda
- Sign-in sheet
- Breaks
- Message and telephone location
- Cell phone policy
- Facilities
- Other concerns

Visual 8:   <u>Sample Agenda</u>

Morning Session
- Unit 1: Course Welcome and ICS Overview (1 hours)
- Unit 2: NIMS Management Characteristics (1.5 hours)
- Unit 3: ICS Functional Areas and Command Staff Roles (1 hour)

Afternoon Session
- Unit 4: General Staff Roles (1 hour)
- Unit 5: How ICS Applies to You (1 hour)
- Final Exam (1 hour)

Visual 9:   <u>Course Completion</u>

In order to successfully complete this course, you must:

- Participate in unit activities.
- Achieve 75% or higher on the final exam.
- Complete the end-of-course evaluation.

Visual 10: Unit 1: ICS Overview

Unit 1 provides an overview of the Incident Command System (ICS). At the end of this lesson, you should be able to:

- Describe the Whole Community approach to ICS.
- Identify the basic concept and benefits of ICS.

Visual 11: <u>Whole Community</u>

Every part of society must be involved in preparing for, protecting against, responding to, recovering from, and mitigating any and all incidents. The Federal Government is only one part of the whole community.

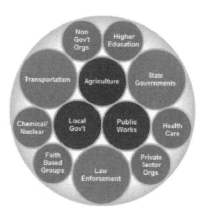

The **Whole Community** approach ensures solutions that serve the entire community are implemented, while simultaneously making sure that the resources the different members of the community bring to the table are used efficiently. These members include those in all levels of government as well as those in non-governmental and private-sector organizations in fields such as transportation, health care, schools, public works, communications, agriculture, chemical/nuclear, and more.

Note

As part of the whole community, you will need to understand your role in the Incident Command System (ICS) and how ICS works to help everyone involved. This course will help in that regard.

This course addresses all disciplines that use ICS across the community. In addition, Unit 4 handouts provide discipline-specific examples of ICS applications, such as Public Works, Schools, and Utilities. Unit 5 incorporates a variety of disciplines in a series of scenarios.

Visual 12:   <u>What is the Incident Command System?</u>

The Incident Command System (ICS) is a standardized approach to incident management that:

- Is used for all kinds of incidents by all types of organizations and at all levels of government; ICS is applicable to small incidents as well as large and complex ones.
- Can be used not only for emergencies, but also for planned events.
- Enables a coordinated response among various jurisdictions and agencies.
- Establishes common processes for incident-level planning and resource management.
- Allows for the integration of resources (such as facilities, equipment, personnel) within a common organizational structure.

Note

ICS - Brief History

ICS was developed in the 1970s following a series of catastrophic fires in California. Property damage ran into the millions, and many people died or were injured.

The personnel assigned to study the case histories and determine the causes of these disasters discovered that response problems could rarely be attributed to lack of resources or failure of tactics.

Visual 13: <u>When is ICS Used?</u>

The Incident Command System (ICS) can be used to manage any type of incident, including a planned event (e.g., the Olympics, the Governor's inauguration, state fairs, a local parade, etc.). The use of ICS is applicable to all types of incidents, regardless of their size or cause.

As a system, ICS is extremely useful. Not only does it provide an organizational structure for incident management, but it also guides the process for planning, building, and adapting that structure.

Using ICS for every incident or planned event provides the practice that will help to maintain and improve skills needed to effectively coordinate larger or more complex efforts.

Visual 14: <u>ICS for Planned Events</u>

From your own experiences, what are some examples of different types of planned events where ICS was used?

Why was it beneficial to use ICS?

Visual 15: <u>Incident Command System:</u>
<u>Promoting Response Partnerships</u>

Video

Incident Command System: Promoting Response Partnerships
The following video will introduce ICS and describe its importance.
Video Duration: 1 minute, 30 seconds

Incident Command System: Promoting Response Partnerships
Video Transcript:

Disaster can strike anytime, anywhere. It takes many forms—a hurricane, an earthquake, a tornado, a flood, a fire or a hazardous spill, or an act of terrorism. An incident can build over days or weeks, or hit suddenly, without warning.

A poorly managed incident response can undermine our safety and wellbeing. With so much at stake, we must effectively manage our response efforts.

Although most incidents are handled locally, partnerships among local, tribal, State, and Federal agencies as well as nongovernmental and private-sector organizations may be required.

As partners, we must respond together in a seamless, coordinated fashion.

The Incident Command System, or ICS, helps ensure integration of our response efforts. ICS is a standardized, on-scene, all-hazards approach to incident management. ICS allows all responders to adopt an integrated organizational structure that matches the complexities and demands of the incident while respecting agency and jurisdictional authorities. Although ICS promotes standardization, it is not without needed flexibility. For example, the ICS organizational structure can expand or contract to meet incident needs.

In this course, you'll learn ICS principles. And more importantly, you'll learn to interface better with your response partners.

Visual 16: <u>ICS as a Component of the National Incident Management System (NIMS)</u>

The National Incident Management System (NIMS) is a systematic, proactive approach to guide all levels of government, nongovernmental organizations (NGOs), and the private sector to work together to prevent, protect against, mitigate, respond to, and recover from the effects of incidents. NIMS provides a consistent foundation for all incidents, ranging from daily occurrences to incidents requiring a coordinated Federal response.

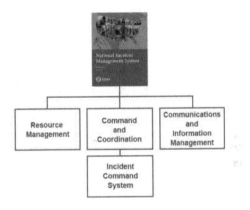

NIMS is organized into three major components:

- Resource Management
- Command and Coordination - including the Incident Command System
- Communications and Information Management

It is important to note that the Incident Command System (ICS) is just one part of NIMS.

Note

National Preparedness and ICS Requirements

Review the following points about the value of using ICS:

- ICS works! It saves lives! Life safety is the top priority for ICS response.
- The use of ICS is a key indicator of National Incident Management System (NIMS) implementation. Jurisdictions that receive some Federal grants such as National Preparedness Grants must demonstrate NIMS implementation. NIMS provides a systematic, proactive approach guiding departments and agencies at all levels of government, the private sector, and nongovernmental

---

organizations to work seamlessly to prevent, protect against, respond to, recover from, and mitigate the effects of incidents, regardless of cause, size, location, or complexity, in order to reduce the loss of life and property, and harm to the environment.

In addition to the NIMS mandate, the following laws require the use of ICS:

- The Superfund Amendments and Reauthorization Act (SARA) of 1986 established Federal regulations for handling hazardous materials. SARA directed the Occupational Safety and Health Administration (OSHA) to establish rules for operations at hazardous materials incidents.
- OSHA rule 1910.120, effective March 6, 1990, requires all organizations that handle hazardous materials to use ICS. The regulation states: "The Incident Command System shall be established by those employers for the incidents that will be under their control and shall interface with other organizations or agencies who may respond to such an incident."

Note that the Environmental Protection Agency (EPA) requires States to use ICS at hazardous materials incidents.

According to the National Integration Center, "institutionalizing the use of ICS" means that government officials, incident managers, and emergency response organizations at all jurisdictional levels must adopt ICS. Actions to institutionalize the use of ICS take place at two levels:

- Policy Level: At the policy level, institutionalizing ICS means government officials (i.e., Governors, mayors, county and city managers, tribal leaders, and others) must:
  - Adopt ICS through executive order, proclamation, or legislation as the jurisdiction's official incident response system; and
  - Direct that incident managers and response organizations in their jurisdictions train, exercise, and use ICS in their response operations.
- Organizational Level: At the organizational/operational level, evidence that incident managers and emergency response organizations are institutionalizing ICS would include the following:
  - ICS is being integrated into functional and system-wide emergency operations policies, plans, and procedures.
  - ICS training is planned or underway for responders, supervisors, and command-level officers.
  - Responders at all levels are participating in and/or coordinating ICS-oriented exercises that involve responders from multiple disciplines and jurisdictions.

Note

National Preparedness and ICS

NIMS represents a core set of doctrine, concepts, principles, terminology, and organizational processes that enables effective, efficient, and collaborative incident management.

- Resource Management: Resource Management describes standard mechanisms to systematically manage resources, including personnel, equipment, supplies, teams, and facilities, both before and during incidents in order to allow organizations to more effectively share resources when needed.
- Command and Coordination: Command and Coordination describes leadership roles, processes, and recommended organizational structures for incident management at the operational and incident support levels and explains how these structures interact to manage incidents effectively and efficiently.
- Communications and Information Management: Communications and Information Management describes systems and methods that help to ensure that incident personnel and other decision makers have the means and information they need to make and communicate decisions.

Visual 17: <u>Incident Response Problems</u>

?

What are some common causes of incident response problems?

Visual 18: <u>ICS Benefits - Student Activity</u>

Activity Purpose: The purpose of this activity is to discuss the benefits of ICS.

Instructions: Follow the steps below to conduct this activity:

1. Divide into groups of five or six.
2. Work as a team to review the scenario presented below.
3. Identify the top three challenges for officials to manage this incident.
4. Write the challenges on chart paper.
5. Discuss how ICS could be used to address these challenges.
6. Select a spokesperson.

Time: 20 minutes (including debrief)

Scenario:

Continuing severe weather is causing widespread damage. There are multiple impacts in the community. Vehicle movement is constrained, some people are stranded and are in need of assistance, there have been impacts on communications and power, and some structures are impacted. 9-1-1 operators are receiving conflicting reports about a number of life-safety needs, including some weather-related injuries and an unverified report of the structural collapse of an assisted living facility.

	ICS BENEFITS - Student Activity
	Activity Purpose: The purpose of this activity is to discuss the benefits of ICS.
	Instructions: Follow the steps below to conduct this activity:
 Activity	1. Divide into groups of five or six. 2. Work as a team to review the scenario presented below. 3. Identify the top three challenges for officials to manage this incident. 4. Write the challenges on chart paper. 5. Discuss how ICS could be used to address these challenges. 6. Select a spokesperson.
	Time: 20 minutes (including debrief)
	Scenario:
	Continuing severe weather is causing widespread damage. There are multiple impacts in the community. Vehicle movement is constrained, some people are stranded and are in need of assistance, there have been impacts on communications and power, and some structures are impacted. 9-1-1 operators are receiving conflicting reports about a number of life-safety needs, including some weather-related injuries and an unverified report of the structural collapse of an assisted living facility.

Discussion Questions:

What are the priorities for the incident?

What are the top three incident management challenges?

How will ICS help to address these challenges?

Visual 19: <u>Benefits of ICS</u>

The Incident Command System (ICS) has positively impacted incident management efforts by:

- Clarifying chain of command and supervision responsibilities to improve accountability.
- Leveraging interoperable communications systems and plain language to improve communications.
- Providing an orderly, systematic planning process.
- Implementing a common, flexible, predesigned management structure.
- Fostering cooperation between diverse disciplines and agencies.

Note

ICS BENEFITS

The Incident Command System (ICS) has positively impacted incident management efforts by:

- Clarifying chain of command and supervision responsibilities to improve accountability.
- Providing an orderly, systematic planning process
- Implementing a common, flexible, predefined management structure.
- Fostering cooperation between diverse disciplines and agencies.

Visual 20: <u>ICS: Built on Best Practices</u>

The Incident Command System (ICS) has been tested for more than 40 years of emergency and nonemergency applications by all levels of government; and in nongovernmental and private-sector organizations. ICS helps to ensure:

- The safety of responders, community members, and others.
- The achievement of incident objectives.
- The efficient use of resources.

Visual 21: <u>Review Questions</u>

Let's review what you have learned in this Unit:

- What is a basic definition of the Incident Command System?
- Is it the same as NIMS?
- What are some situations for which it can be used?

Visual 22: <u>Unit 1 Summary</u>

You have completed the Course Welcome and Incident Command System (ICS) Overview unit. This unit presented the following key points:

- ICS is a standardized management tool that allows better coordination and use of resources.
- ICS represents organizational "best practices" and has become the standard for emergency management.
- ICS can be used to manage the response for all incidents and planned events.

ICS works! It saves lives!

IS-100.c GLOSSARY

Glossary

Glossary A-I

Access and Functional Needs: Individual circumstances requiring assistance, accommodation, or modification for mobility, communication, transportation, safety, health maintenance, etc., due to any temporary or permanent situation that limits an individual's ability to take action in an emergency.

Agency: A government element with a specific function offering a particular kind of assistance.

Agency Administrator/Executive: The official responsible for administering policy for an agency or jurisdiction.

Agency Representative: A person assigned by a primary, assisting, or cooperating local, state, tribal, territorial, or Federal Government agency, or nongovernmental or private organization, who has authority to make decisions affecting that agency's or organization's participation in incident management activities following appropriate consultation with that agency's leadership.

Area Command: An organization that oversees the management of multiple incidents or oversees the management of a very large or evolving situation with multiple ICS organizations. See *Unified Area Command*.

Assigned Resource: A resource that has been checked in and assigned work tasks on an incident.

Assignment: A task given to a person or team to perform based on operational objectives defined in the IAP.

Assistant: A title for subordinates of principal Command Staff and EOC director's staff positions. The title indicates a level of technical capability, qualification, and responsibility subordinate to the primary positions. Assistants may also be assigned to unit leaders.

Assisting Agency: An agency or organization providing personnel, services, or other resources to the agency with direct responsibility for incident management.

Authority Having Jurisdiction: An entity that has the authority and responsibility for developing, implementing, maintaining, and overseeing the qualification process within its organization or jurisdiction. This may be a state or Federal agency, training commission, NGO, private sector company, or a tribal or local agency such as a police, fire, or public works department. In some cases, the AHJ may provide support to multiple disciplines that collaborate as a part of a team (e.g., an IMT).

Available Resource: A resource assigned to an incident, checked in, and available for assignment.

Badging: The assignment of physical incident-specific credentials to establish legitimacy and permit access to incident sites. See *Credentialing*.

Base: See *Incident Base*.

Branch: The organizational level having functional or geographical responsibility for major aspects of incident operations. A branch falls between the Section Chief and the division or group in the Operations Section, and between the section and units in the Logistics Section. Branches are identified by Roman numerals or by functional area.

Camp: A geographical site within the general incident area (separate from the Incident Base) that is equipped and staffed to provide sleeping, food, water, and sanitary services to incident personnel.

Certification: The process of authoritatively attesting that individuals meet qualifications established for key incident management functions and are, therefore, qualified for specific positions.

Chain of Command: The orderly line of authority within the ranks of incident management organizations.

Check-In: The process through which resources first report to an incident. All responders, regardless of agency affiliation, report in to receive an assignment in accordance with the Incident Commander or Unified Command's established procedures.

Chief: The ICS title for individuals responsible for the management of functional sections: Operations, Planning, Logistics, and Finance/Administration.

Clear Text: Communication that does not use codes. See *Plain Language*.

Command: The act of directing, ordering, or controlling by virtue of explicit statutory, regulatory, or delegated authority.

Command Staff: A group of incident personnel that the Incident Commander or Unified Command assigns to support the command function at an ICP. Command staff often include a PIO, a Safety Officer, and a Liaison Officer, who have assistants as necessary. Additional positions may be needed, depending on the incident.

Cooperating Agency: An agency supplying assistance other than direct operational or support functions or resources to the incident management effort.

Coordinate: To exchange information systematically among principals who have or may have a need to know certain information to carry out specific incident management responsibilities.

Core Capability: An element defined in the National Preparedness Goal as necessary to prevent, protect against, mitigate, respond to, and recover from the threats and hazards that pose the greatest risk.

Credentialing: Providing documentation that identifies personnel and authenticates and verifies their qualification for a particular position. See *Badging*.

Critical Infrastructure: Assets, systems, and networks, whether physical or virtual, so vital to the United States that the incapacitation or destruction of such assets, systems, or networks would have a debilitating impact on security, national economic security, national public health or safety, or any combination of those matters.

Delegation of Authority: A statement that the agency executive delegating authority and assigning responsibility provides to the Incident Commander. The delegation of authority can include priorities, expectations, constraints, and other considerations or guidelines, as needed.

Demobilization: The orderly, safe, and efficient return of an incident resource to its original location and status.

Departmental Operations Center: An operations or coordination center dedicated to a single, specific department or agency. The focus of a DOC is on internal agency incident management and response. DOCs are often linked to and/or physically represented in a combined agency EOC by an authorized agent(s) for the department or agency.

Deputy: A fully qualified individual who, in the absence of a superior, can be delegated the authority to manage a functional operation or to perform a specific task. In some cases, a deputy can act as relief for a superior, and, therefore, should be fully qualified in the position. Deputies generally can be assigned to the Incident Commander, EOC director, General Staff, and branch directors.

Director: The ICS title for individuals responsible for supervision of a branch. Also, an organizational title for an individual responsible for managing and directing the team in an EOC.

Dispatch: The ordered movement of a resource or resources to an assigned operational mission, or an administrative move from one location to another.

Division: The organizational level having responsibility for operations within a defined geographic area. Divisions are established when the number of resources exceeds the manageable span of control of the Section Chief. See *Group*.

Emergency: Any incident, whether natural, technological, or human-caused, that necessitates responsive action to protect life or property.

Emergency Management Assistance Compact: A congressionally ratified agreement that provides form and structure to interstate mutual aid. Through EMAC, a disaster-affected state can request and receive assistance from other member states quickly and efficiently, resolving two key issues up front: liability and reimbursement.

Emergency Operations Center: The physical location where the coordination of information and resources to support incident management (on-scene operations) activities normally takes place. An EOC may be a temporary facility or located in a more central or permanently established facility, perhaps at a higher level of organization within a jurisdiction.

Emergency Operations Plan: A plan for responding to a variety of potential hazards.

Emergency Support Function: The grouping of governmental and certain private sector capabilities into an organizational structure to provide capabilities and services most likely needed to manage domestic incidents.

Essential Elements of Information: Important and standard information items, which support timely and informed decisions.

Evacuation: The organized, phased, and supervised withdrawal, dispersal, or removal of people from dangerous or potentially dangerous areas, and their reception and care in safe areas.

Event: See *Planned Event*.

Federal: Of or pertaining to the Federal Government of the United States.

Finance/Administration Section: The ICS Section responsible for an incident's administrative and financial considerations.

General Staff: A group of incident personnel organized according to function and reporting to the Incident Commander or Unified Command. The ICS General Staff consists of the Operations Section Chief, Planning Section Chief, Logistics Section Chief, Finance/Administration Section Chief.

Group: An organizational subdivision established to divide the incident management structure into functional areas of operation. Groups are composed of resources assembled to perform a special function not necessarily within a single geographic area. See *Division*.

Hazard: Something potentially dangerous or harmful, often the root cause of an unwanted outcome.

Incident: An occurrence, natural or manmade, that necessitates a response to protect life or property. In this document, the word "incident" includes planned events as well as emergencies and/or disasters of all kinds and sizes.

Incident Action Plan: An oral or written plan containing the objectives established by the Incident Commander or Unified

Command and addressing tactics and support activities for the planned operational period, generally 12 to 24 hours.

Incident Base: A location where personnel coordinate and administer logistics functions for an incident. There is typically only one base per incident. (An incident name or other designator is added to the term *Base*.) The ICP may be co-located with the Incident Base.

Incident Command: The ICS organizational element responsible for overall management of the incident and consisting of the Incident Commander or Unified Command and any additional Command Staff activated.

Incident Command Post: The field location where the primary functions of incident command are performed. The ICP may be co-located with the Incident Base or other incident facilities.

Incident Command System: A standardized approach to the command, control, and coordination of on-scene incident management, providing a common hierarchy within which personnel from multiple organizations can be effective. ICS is the combination of procedures, personnel, facilities, equipment, and communications operating within a common organizational structure, designed to aid in the management of on-scene resources during incidents. It is used for all kinds of incidents and is applicable to small, as well as large and complex, incidents, including planned events.

Incident Commander: The individual responsible for on-scene incident activities, including developing incident objectives and ordering and releasing resources. The Incident Commander has overall authority and responsibility for conducting incident operations.

Incident Complex: Two or more individual incidents located in the same general area and assigned to a single Incident Commander or Unified Command.

Incident Management: The broad spectrum of activities and organizations providing operations, coordination, and support applied at all levels of government, using both governmental and nongovernmental resources to plan for, respond to, and recover from an incident, regardless of cause, size, or complexity.

Incident Management Assistance Team: A team of ICS-qualified personnel, configured according to ICS, that deploy in support of affected jurisdictions and/or on-scene personnel.

Incident Management Team: A rostered group of ICS-qualified personnel consisting of an Incident Commander, Command and General Staff, and personnel assigned to other key ICS positions.

Incident Objective: A statement of an outcome to be accomplished or achieved. Incident objectives are used to select strategies and tactics. Incident objectives should be realistic, achievable, and measurable, yet flexible enough to allow strategic and tactical alternatives.

Incident Personnel: All individuals who have roles in incident management or support, whether on scene, in an EOC, or participating in a MAC Group.

Information Management: The collection, organization, and control over the structure, processing, and delivery of information from one or more sources and distribution to one or more audiences who have a stake in that information.

Intelligence/Investigations Function: Efforts to determine the source or cause of the incident (e.g., disease outbreak, fire, complex coordinated attack, or cyber incident) in order to control its impact and/or help prevent the occurrence of similar incidents. In ICS, the function may be accomplished in the Planning Section, Operations Section, Command Staff, as a separate General Staff section, or in some combination of these locations.

Interoperability: The ability of systems, personnel, and equipment to provide and receive functionality, data, information, and/or services to and from other systems, personnel, and equipment, between both public and private agencies, departments, and other organizations, in a manner enabling them to operate effectively together.

Glossary

Glossary J-P

Joint Field Office: The primary Federal incident management field structure. The JFO is a temporary Federal facility that provides a central location for the coordination of local, state, tribal, and Federal governments and private sector and NGOs with primary responsibility for response and recovery.

Joint Information Center: A facility in which personnel coordinate incident-related public information activities. The JIC serves as the central point of contact for all news media. Public information officials from all participating agencies co-locate at, or virtually coordinate through, the JIC.

Joint Information System: A structure that integrates overarching incident information and public affairs into a cohesive organization designed to provide consistent, coordinated, accurate, accessible, timely, and complete information during crisis or incident operations.

Jurisdiction: Jurisdiction has two definitions depending on the context:

•*A range or sphere of authority*. Public agencies have jurisdiction at an incident related to their legal responsibilities and authority.

Jurisdictional authority at an incident can be political or geographical (e.g., local, state, tribal, territorial, and Federal boundary lines) and/or functional (e.g., law enforcement, public health).

•*A political subdivision* (e.g., municipality, county, parish, state, Federal) with the responsibility for ensuring public safety, health, and welfare within its legal authorities and geographic boundaries.

Kind: As applied to incident resources, a class or group of items or people of the same nature or character or classified together because they have traits in common.

Leader: The ICS title for an individual who is responsible for supervision of a unit, strike team, resource team, or task force.

Liaison Officer: A member of the ICS Command Staff responsible for coordinating with representatives from cooperating and assisting agencies or organizations.

Local Government: Public entities responsible for the security and welfare of a designated area as established by law. A county, municipality, city, town, township, local public authority, school district, special district, intrastate district, council of governments (regardless of whether the council of governments is incorporated as a nonprofit corporation under state law), regional or interstate government entity, or agency or instrumentality of a local government; a tribe or authorized tribal entity, or in Alaska, a Native Village or Alaska Regional Native Corporation; a rural community, unincorporated town or village, or other public entity.

Logistics: The process and procedure for providing resources and other services to support incident management.

Logistics Section: The ICS Section responsible for providing facilities, services, and material support for the incident.

Management by Objectives: A management approach, fundamental to NIMS, that involves (1) establishing objectives, e.g., specific, measurable and realistic outcomes to be achieved;(2) identifying strategies, tactics, and tasks to achieve the objectives; (3) performing the tactics and tasks and measuring and documenting results in achieving the objectives; and (4) taking corrective action to modify strategies, tactics, and/or performance to achieve the objectives.

Manager: The individual within an ICS organizational unit assigned specific managerial responsibilities (e.g., Staging Area Manager or Camp Manager).

Mission Area: One of five areas (Prevention, Protection, Mitigation, Response, and Recovery) designated in the National Preparedness Goal to group core capabilities.

Mitigation: The capabilities necessary to reduce the loss of life and property from natural and/or manmade disasters by lessening the impacts of disasters.

Mobilization: The processes and procedures for activating, assembling, and transporting resources that have been requested to respond to or support an incident.

Multiagency Coordination Group: A group, typically consisting of agency administrators or executives from organizations, or their designees, that provides policy guidance to incident personnel, supports resource prioritization and allocation, and enables decision making among elected and appointed officials and senior executives in other organizations, as well as those directly responsible for incident management.

Multiagency Coordination System: An overarching term for the NIMS Command and Coordination systems: ICS, EOCs, MAC Group/policy groups, and JISs.

Mutual Aid Agreement or Assistance Agreement: A written or oral agreement between and among agencies/organizations and/or jurisdictions that provides a mechanism to quickly obtain assistance in the form of personnel, equipment, materials, and other associated services. The primary objective is to facilitate the rapid, short-term deployment of support prior to, during, and/or after an incident.

National: Of a nationwide character, including the local, state, tribal, territorial, and Federal aspects of governance and policy.

National Incident Management System: A systematic, proactive approach to guide all levels of government, NGOs, and the private sector to work together to prevent, protect against, mitigate, respond to, and recover from the effects of incidents. NIMS provides stakeholders across the whole community with the shared vocabulary, systems, and processes to successfully deliver the capabilities described in the National Preparedness System. NIMS provides a consistent foundation for dealing with all incidents, ranging from daily occurrences to incidents requiring a coordinated Federal response.

National Planning Frameworks: Guidance documents for each of the five preparedness mission areas that describe how the whole community works together to achieve the National Preparedness Goal. The Frameworks foster a shared understanding of roles and responsibilities, from the firehouse to the White House, and clarifies how the Nation coordinates, shares information, and works together— ultimately resulting in a more secure and resilient Nation.

National Preparedness: The actions taken to plan, organize, equip, train, and exercise to build and sustain the capabilities necessary to prevent, protect against, mitigate the effects of, respond to, and recover from those threats that pose the greatest risk to the security of the Nation.

National Preparedness Goal: Doctrine describing what it means for the whole community to be prepared for the types of incidents that pose the greatest threat to the security of the Nation, including acts of terrorism and emergencies and disasters, regardless of cause. The goal itself is: "A secure and resilient Nation with the capabilities required across the whole community to prevent, protect against, mitigate, respond to, and recover from the threats and hazards that pose the greatest risk."

National Preparedness System: An organized process to achieve the National Preparedness Goal of a secure and resilient Nation.

National Response Coordination Center: A multiagency coordination center located at FEMA Headquarters. Its staff coordinates the overall Federal support for major disasters and emergencies, including catastrophic incidents and emergency management program implementation.

Nongovernmental Organization: A group that is based on the interests of its members, individuals, or institutions. An NGO is not created by a government, but it may work cooperatively with government. Examples of NGOs include faith-based groups, relief agencies, organizations that support people with access and functional needs, and animal welfare organizations.

Normal Operations/Steady State: The activation level that describes routine monitoring of jurisdictional situation (no event or incident anticipated).

Officer: The ICS title for a member of the Command Staff authorized to make decisions and take action related to his/her area of responsibility.

Operational Period: The time scheduled for executing a given set of operation actions, as specified in the IAP. Operational periods can be of various lengths, but are typically 12 to 24 hours.

Operational Security: The implementation of procedures and activities to protect sensitive or classified operations involving sources and methods of intelligence collection, investigative techniques, tactical actions, counter surveillance measures, counterintelligence methods, undercover officers, cooperating witnesses, and informants.

Operations Section: The ICS Section responsible for implementing tactical incident operations described in the IAP. In ICS, the Operations Section may include subordinate branches, divisions, and/or groups.

Organization: Any association or group of persons with like objectives. Examples include, but are not limited to, governmental departments and agencies, NGOs, and private sector entities.

Plain Language: Communication that the intended audience can understand and that meets the communicator's purpose. For the purpose of NIMS, plain language refers to a communication style that avoids or limits the use of codes, abbreviations, and jargon, as appropriate, during incidents involving more than a single agency.

Planned Event (Event): An incident that is a scheduled non-emergency activity (e.g., sporting event, concert, parade).

Planning Meeting: A meeting held, as needed, before and throughout an incident to select specific strategies and tactics for incident control operations and for service and support planning.

Planning Section: The ICS Section that collects, evaluates, and disseminates operational information related to the incident and for the preparation and documentation of the IAP. This section also maintains information on the current and forecasted situation and on the status of resources assigned to the incident.

Position Qualifications: The minimum criteria necessary for individuals to fill a specific position.

Prevention: The capabilities necessary to avoid, prevent, or stop a threatened or actual act of terrorism. In national preparedness guidance, the term "prevention" refers to preventing imminent threats.

Private Sector: Organizations and individuals that are not part of any governmental structure. The private sector includes for-profit and not-for-profit organizations, formal and informal structures, commerce, and industry.

Protection: The capabilities necessary to secure the homeland against acts of terrorism and manmade or natural disasters.

Protocol: A set of established guidelines for actions (designated by individuals, teams, functions, or capabilities) under various specified conditions.

Public Information: Processes, procedures, and systems for communicating timely, accurate, and accessible information on an incident's cause, size, and current situation; resources committed; and other matters of general interest to the public, responders, and additional stakeholders (both directly affected and indirectly affected).

Public Information Officer: A member of the ICS Command Staff responsible for interfacing with the public and media and/or with other agencies with incident-related information needs.

Glossary

Glossary Q-Z

Recovery: The capabilities necessary to assist communities affected by an incident to recover effectively.

Recovery Plan: A plan to restore an incident-affected area or community.

Recovery Support Function: Organizing structures for key functional areas of assistance outlined in the National Disaster Recovery Framework that group capabilities of various government and private sector partner organizations to promote effective recovery from disasters before and after disasters strike.

Reimbursement: A mechanism to recoup funds expended for incident-specific activities.

Resource Management: Systems for identifying available resources at all jurisdictional levels to enable timely, efficient, and unimpeded access to resources needed to prepare for, respond to, or recover from an incident.

Resource Team: See *Strike Team*.

Resource Tracking: The process that all incident personnel and staff from associated organizations use to maintain information regarding the location and status of resources ordered for, deployed to, or assigned to an incident.

Resources: Personnel, equipment, teams, supplies, and facilities available or potentially available for assignment to incident operations and for which status is maintained. Resources are described by kind and type and may be used in operational support or supervisory capacities at an incident or at an EOC.

Response: The capabilities necessary to save lives, protect property and the environment, and meet basic human needs after an incident has occurred.

Safety Officer: In ICS, a member of the Command Staff responsible for monitoring incident operations and advising the Incident Commander or Unified Command on all matters relating to operational safety, including the health and safety of incident personnel. The Safety Officer modifies or stops the work of personnel to prevent unsafe acts.

Section: The ICS organizational element having responsibility for a major functional area of incident management (e.g., Operations, Planning, Logistics, and Finance/Administration).

Single Resource: An individual, a piece of equipment and its personnel complement, or a crew/team of individuals with an identified work supervisor that can be used on an incident.

Situation Report: Confirmed or verified information regarding the specific details relating to an incident.

Span of Control: The number of subordinates for which a supervisor is responsible, usually expressed as the ratio of supervisors to individuals.

Staging Area: A temporary location for available resources in which personnel, supplies, and equipment await operational assignment.

Standard Operating Procedure: A reference document or an operations manual that provides the purpose, authorities, duration, and details for the preferred method of performing a single function or several interrelated functions in a uniform manner.

State: Used in this document to include any state of the United States, the District of Columbia, the Commonwealth of Puerto Rico, the Virgin Islands, Guam, American Samoa, the Commonwealth of the Northern Mariana Islands, and any possession of the United States.

Status Report: Reports, such as spot reports, that include vital and/or time-sensitive information. Status reports are typically function-specific, less formal than situation reports, and are not always issued on a specific schedule.

Strategy: The general course of action or direction to accomplish incident objectives.

Strike Team: A set number of resources of the same kind and type that have an established minimum number of personnel, common communications, and a leader. In the law enforcement community, strike teams are referred to as resource teams.

Supervisor: The ICS title for an individual responsible for a division or group.

System: Any combination of processes, facilities, equipment, personnel, procedures, and communications integrated for a specific purpose.

Tactics: The deployment and directing of resources on an incident to accomplish the objectives.

Task Force: Any combination of resources of different kinds and/or types assembled to support a specific mission or operational need.

Terrorism: Any activity that involves an act that is dangerous to human life or potentially destructive of critical infrastructure and is a violation of the criminal laws of the United States or of any state or other subdivision of the United States; and appears to be intended to intimidate or coerce a civilian population, or to influence the policy of a government by intimidation or coercion, or to affect the conduct of a government by mass destruction, assassination, or kidnapping.

Threat: A natural or manmade occurrence, an individual, an entity, or an action having or indicating the potential to harm life, information, operations, the environment, and/or property.

Tools: Instruments and capabilities that allow the professional performance of tasks, such as information systems, agreements, doctrine, capabilities, and legislative authorities.

Type: A NIMS resource classification that refers to capability of a specific kind of resource to which a metric is applied to designate it as a specific numbered class.

Unified Area Command: A version of command established when incidents under an Area Command are multijurisdictional. See *Area Command*.

Unified Command: An ICS application used when more than one agency has incident jurisdiction or when incidents cross political jurisdictions.

Unit: The organizational element with functional responsibility for a specific activity within the Planning, Logistics, and Finance/Administration Sections in ICS.

Unit Leader: The individual in charge of a unit in ICS.

United States National Grid: A point and area location reference system that FEMA and other incident management organizations use as an accurate and expeditious alternative to latitude/longitude.

Unity of Command: A NIMS guiding principle stating that each individual involved in incident management reports to and takes direction from only one person.

Unity of Effort: A NIMS guiding principle that provides coordination through cooperation and common interests and does not interfere with Federal department and agency supervisory, command, or statutory authorities.

Whole Community: A focus on enabling the participation in incident management activities of a wide range of players from the private and nonprofit sectors, including NGOs and the general public, in conjunction with the participation of all levels of government, to foster better coordination and working relationships.

Lesson 2: NIMS Management Characteristics

Visual 1:   <u>Unit 2 Overview</u>

This unit presents the National Incident Management System
(NIMS) management characteristics. These characteristics are the foundation of all
NIMS command and coordination components, including the Incident Command
System (ICS).

Objective:

At the end of this unit, you should be able to:

- Describe the 14 NIMS management characteristics.

Visual 2:   <u>Making ICS Work</u>

Effective incident management relies on a common organizational structure for managing resources, making decisions, and assigning tasks. The Incident Command System (ICS) uses a standardized management approach to ensure that incidents are properly managed and communications are effectively coordinated during an incident.

As an incident occurs, you may be called upon to assist -- making you a part of this organizational structure. To ensure success, you should understand how this structure works.

Visual 3:   NIMS Management Characteristics:
Overview

	NIMS Management Characteristics
	The following video will introduce the NIMS Management Characteristics discussed in detail in this unit.
Video	Video Duration: 2 minutes, 30 seconds

NIMS Management Characteristics: Overview

Video Transcript

As you learned in the previous lesson, ICS is based on proven NIMS management principles, which contribute to the strength and efficiency of the overall system.

ICS incorporates a wide range of management features and principles, beginning with the use of common terminology.

[David Burns, Emergency Preparedness Manager, University of California Los Angeles] Communication is probably one of the most essential elements of ICS. It's important that we know how to communicate.

[Daryl Lee Spiewak, Former Emergency Programs Manager, the Brazos River Authority] If the terms that I use mean different things to different people, we're going to have a hard time communicating and doing what needs to be done to accomplish our mission.

ICS emphasizes effective planning, including management by objectives and reliance on an Incident Action Plan.

[Roberta Runge, EPA National NIMS Coordinator] You have to coordinate on what your end objective is. All up and down the chain you have to have a common end goal. So you can establish your objectives, you can ensure they're in the Incident Action Plan, and you can ensure that they are in agreement.

ICS employs a modular organizational structure that can be tailored based on the size, complexity and hazards of an incident. Command of this organization is established under a single Incident Commander or a Unified Command.

The ICS features related to command structure include chain of command and unity of command.

[Bill Campbell, Former Director of Training, New York State Emergency Management Office] One of the benefits is it gets all of the different organizations working under the same framework.

ICS helps ensure full utilization of all incident resources by:

- Maintaining a manageable span of control
- Establishing designated incident facilities and locations
- Implementing comprehensive resource management practices
- Defining clear processes for dispatch/ deployment of resources
- Ensuring integrated communications

ICS supports responders and decision makers through effective information and intelligence management.

[Kristy Plourde, Emergency Management Specialist, U.S. Coast Guard] The common operating picture is a critical thing that the Coast Guard has been working hard on recently for ourselves because it's something that helps us maintain a better operational picture and it's more consistent across the board, everyone up and down the chain of command and across to other agencies understand the same picture.

ICS counts on each of us taking personal accountability for our own actions. And finally, the mobilization process helps ensure that incident objectives can be achieved while responders remain safe.

[Kristy Plourde, Emergency Management Specialist, U.S. Coast Guard] To have NIMS work effectively, it's got to be top-down support.

The NIMS Management Characteristics covered in this lesson form the basis for effective, team-based incident response under the Incident Command System (ICS).

Visual 4:   NIMS Management Characteristics:
Overview

The Incident Command System (ICS) is based on the following 14 proven NIMS management characteristics, each of which contributes to the strength and efficiency of the overall system:

• Common Terminology • Modular Organization • Management by Objectives • Incident Action Planning • Manageable Span of Control • Incident Facilities and Locations • Comprehensive Resource Management	• Integrated Communications • Establishment and Transfer of Command • Unified Command • Chain of Command and Unity of Command • Accountability • Dispatch/Deployment • Information and Intelligence Management

Visual 5:   <u>Common Terminology</u>

The Incident Command System (ICS) establishes Common Terminology that allows diverse incident management and support organizations to work together across a wide variety of emergency functions and hazard scenarios. This common terminology covers the following:

- **Organizational Functions:** Major functions and functional units with incident management responsibilities are named and defined. They remain standard and consistent.
- **Resource Descriptions:** Major resources – including personnel, equipment, teams, and facilities – are given common names and are "typed" with respect to their capabilities.
- **Incident Facilities:** Common terminology is used to designate the facilities in the vicinity of the incident area.

During an incident:

- Communications should use common terms.
- Organizations should avoid radio codes, agency-specific codes, acronyms, or jargon. Usage of these types of codes may cause confusion or possibly compromise life safety due to a misunderstanding or misinterpretation.

The goal is to promote understanding among all parties involved in managing an incident.

Visual 6:   Common Terminology Discussion

Even if you use codes on a daily basis, why should you use common terminology during an incident response?

Visual 7: <u>Modular Organization</u>

The Incident Command System (ICS) organizational structure develops in a modular fashion based on the incident's size and complexity.

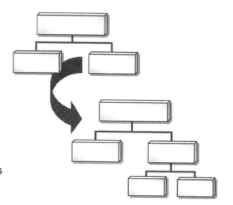

- The responsibility for the establishment and expansion of the ICS modular organization rests with the Incident Commander.
- As the incident grows more complex, the ICS organization may expand as functional responsibilities are delegated.

 Note	***ICS Organizational Structure*** The ICS organizational structure develops in a top-down, modular fashion that is based on the size and complexity of the incident, as well as the specifics of the hazard environment created by the incident. As incident complexity increases, the organization expands from the top down as functional responsibilities are delegated. The ICS organizational structure is flexible. When needed, separate functional elements can be established and subdivided to enhance internal organizational management and external coordination. As the ICS organizational structure expands, the number of management positions also expands to adequately address the requirements of the incident.

Visual 8: <u>**Management by Objectives**</u>

The Incident Commander or Unified
Command (which will be discussed
later), establishes incident objectives
that drive incident operations.

Management by Objectives includes
the following:

- Establishing specific, measurable
  incident objectives.
- Identifying strategies, tactics, tasks
  and activities to achieve the
  objectives.
- Developing and issuing
  assignments, plans, procedures,
  and protocols to accomplish
  identified tasks.
- Documenting results for the incident
  objectives.

Visual 9:   <u>Incident Action Planning</u>

Incident action planning guides effective incident management activities. An Incident Action Plan (IAP) is a concise, coherent means of capturing and communicating overall incident priorities, objectives, strategies, tactics, and assignments in the context of both operational and support activities. The IAP should focus on addressing the needs of future timeframes (called operational periods).

Incident Action Plan

* What do we need to do?

* Who is responsible for doing it?

* What resources are needed?

* How do we communicate?

To be effective, an IAP should:

* Cover a specified timeframe
* Be proactive
* Specify the incident objectives
* State the activities to be completed
* Assign responsibilities
* Identify needed resources
* Specify communication protocols

For smaller/less complex incidents, the IAP may be oral or written, except for hazardous materials incidents, which require a written IAP. FEMA has developed a series of ICS Forms for use in developing a written IAP.

Note

Incident Action Plan

Every response has a strategy—like a lesson plan—called an Incident Action Plan (IAP).

To be effective, an IAP should:

* Cover a specified timeframe
* Be proactive
* Specify the incident objectives
* State the activities to be completed
* Assign responsibilities
* Identify needed resources
* Specify communication protocols

Even the smallest of incidents are managed by incident objectives and plans. The plan can be as simple as the next steps the Incident

---

> Commander plans to do. The steps can be orally communicated to
> the rest of the ICS organization.

Note

Incident Action Plan Questions

Every IAP must answer the following four questions:

- What do we want to do?
- Who is responsible for doing it?
- How do we communicate with each other?
- What is the procedure if someone is injured?

Visual 10:   Incident Action Plan - Activity 2.1

Activity Purpose: To illustrate how to develop an IAP.

Instructions: Working in groups:

1. Identify four items you would include in an Incident Action Plan for the severe weather scenario described below.
2. Record these four IAP items on chart paper.
3. Select a spokesperson to report back to the group. Be prepared to share your answers in 5 minutes.

Time: 10 minutes

Scenario: Continuing severe weather is causing widespread damage. There are multiple impacts in the community. Vehicle movement is constrained, some people are stranded and are in need of assistance, there have been impacts on communications and power, and some structures are impacted. 9-1-1 operators are receiving conflicting reports about a number of life-safety needs, including some weather-related injuries and an unverified report of the structural collapse of an assisted living facility.

 Activity	**Incident Action Plan - Activity 2.1 - SM** Activity Purpose: To illustrate how to develop an IAP. Instructions: Working in groups: 1. Identify four items you would include in an Incident Action Plan for the severe weather scenario described below. 2. Record these four IAP items on chart paper. 3. Select a spokesperson to report back to the group. Be prepared to share your answers in 5 minutes. Time: 10 minutes Scenario: Continuing severe weather is causing widespread damage. There are multiple impacts in the community. Vehicle movement is constrained, some people are stranded and are in need of assistance, there have been impacts on communications and power, and some structures are impacted. 9-1-1 operators are receiving conflicting reports about a number of life-safety needs, including some weather-related injuries and an unverified report of the structural collapse of an assisted living facility.

Visual 11: <u>Manageable Span of Control</u>

Depending on your role within the Incident Command System (ICS) structure, you may be asked to manage the activities of others.

Span of control refers to the number of individuals or resources that one supervisor can manage effectively during an incident.

The optimal span of control is one supervisor to five subordinates (1:5).

However, effective incident management may require ratios significantly different from this. This ratio is a guideline--incident personnel should use their best judgement to determine the appropriate ratio for an incident.

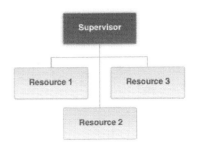

Note	If too much responsibility is given to the supervisor, the span of control may become unmanageable. A manageable span of control on incidents may actually vary depending upon the type of incident, nature of the task, hazards and safety factors, and distances between personnel and resources.
	Maintaining a manageable span of control is particularly important at incidents where safety and accountability are a top priority.

Visual 12: Manageable Span of Control
Discussion

?

What are some examples of when span of control is most critical?

Visual 13: <u>Incident Facilities and Locations</u>

Depending upon the incident size and complexity, various types of support facilities may be established by Incident Command. These designated facilities typically include:

- Incident Command Post (ICP)
- Incident base, staging areas, and camps
- Mass casualty triage areas
- Point-of-distribution
- Emergency shelters

Visual 14: Comprehensive Resource Management

Comprehensive Resource Management describes standard mechanisms to identify requirements, order and acquire, mobilize, track and report, demobilize, and reimburse and restock resources such as personnel, teams, facilities, equipment and supplies.

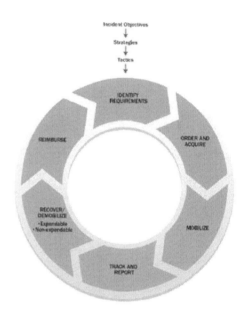

 Note	Key resource management activities include: • Resource Identification and Typing • Qualification, Certification and Credentialing Personnel • Planning for Resources • Acquiring, Storing and Inventorying Resources

Visual 15: <u>Comprehensive Resource</u>
<u>Management Discussion</u>

?

Why is Comprehensive Resource Management important during an incident?

Visual 16: <u>Integrated Communications</u>

Incident communications are facilitated through the development and use of a common communications plan and interoperable communication processes and systems that include voice and data links.

Integrated Communications are necessary to:

- Maintain connectivity
- Achieve situational awareness
- Facilitate information sharing

Visual 17: <u>Integrated</u>
<u>Communications Discussion</u>

?

What are some examples of what Integrated Communications may look like?

Visual 18: Establishment and Transfer of Command

The command function should be clearly established at the beginning of an incident. The jurisdiction or organization with primary responsibility for the incident designates the Incident Commander and the process for transferring command.

Transfer of command may occur during the course of an incident. When command is transferred, the process should include a briefing that captures all essential information for continuing safe and effective operations.

Visual 19: <u>Establishment and Transfer of</u> <u>Command Discussion</u>

?

What are some reasons that Command might be transferred?

Visual 20: <u>Unified Command</u>

In a Unified Command there is no single "Commander." Instead the Unified Command manages the incident through jointly approved objectives. Unified Command allows agencies with different legal, geographic, and functional responsibilities to work together effectively without affecting individual agency authority, responsibility, or accountability.

Unified Command is typically established when no single jurisdiction, agency or organization has the authority and/or resources to manage the incident on its own.

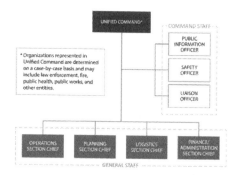

Visual 21: <u>Chain of Command</u>

Chain of command is an orderly line that details how authority flows through the hierarchy of the incident management organization. Chain of command:

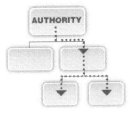

- Allows an Incident Commander to direct and control the actions of all personnel on the incident.
- Avoids confusion by requiring that orders flow from supervisors.

Visual 22: <u>Unity of Command</u>

While chain of command relates to the overall hierarchy of the organization, unity of command deals with the fact that all individuals have a single designated supervisor they report to.

Based on the principle of unity of command, you will:

- Report to only one Incident Command System (ICS) supervisor.
- Receive work assignments only from your ICS supervisor.

When you are assigned to an incident, you no longer report directly to your day-to-day supervisor.

Visual 23: <u>Accountability</u>

Effective accountability during incident operations is essential. As part of the Incident Command System (ICS) structure, you will need to abide by agency policies and guidelines and any applicable local, tribal, state, or Federal rules and regulations.

There are several principles you will need to adhere to:

- **Check-In/Check-Out.** All responders must report in to receive an assignment. Checking out is just as critical as checking in.
- **Incident Action Planning.** Response operations must be coordinated as outlined in the Incident Action Plan.
- **Unity of Command.** Each individual will be assigned to only one supervisor.
- **Personal Responsibility.** ICS relies on each individual taking personal accountability for his or her own actions.
- **Span of Control.** Supervisors must be able to adequately supervise and control their subordinates, as well as communicate with and manage all resources under their supervision.
- **Resource Tracking.** Supervisors must record and report resource status changes as they occur. Accountability starts as soon as a resource is requested through the time that the resource returns to their home base safely.

Visual 24: <u>Dispatch/Deployment</u>

Resources should be deployed only when requested or when dispatched by an appropriate authority through established resource management systems.

Resources not requested should refrain from self-dispatching to avoid overburdening the incident command.

 Note	**Dispatch/Deployment** Another key feature of ICS is the importance of managing resources to adjust to changing conditions. When an incident occurs, you must be dispatched or deployed to become part of the incident response. In other words, until you are deployed to the incident organization, you remain in your everyday role. After being deployed, your first task is to check in and receive an assignment. After check-in, you will locate your incident supervisor and obtain your initial briefing. The briefings you receive and give should include: • Current assessment of the situation. • Identification of your specific job responsibilities. • Identification of coworkers. • Location of work area. • Identification of break areas, as appropriate. • Procedural instructions for obtaining needed resources. • Operational periods/work shifts. • Required safety procedures and personal protective equipment (PPE), as appropriate.

Visual 25: <u>Dispatch/Deployment - Activity 2.2</u>

  Activity	***Dispatch/Deployment - Activity 2.2*** Instructions: Working individually: • Review the scenario and discussion question presented in the Student Manual. • Be prepared to share your answer in 5 minutes. Time: 10 minutes Scenario: Rosa is an off-duty certified Emergency Medical Technician who lives near the scene of a major structural collapse that has occurred in a busy shopping center. The media are reporting that there are injured people wandering around the parking area who need immediate medical attention. **What should Rosa do?**

Visual 26: <u>Dispatch/Deployment Discussion</u>

Why shouldn't personnel arrive at an incident without being requested or dispatched?

Visual 27: Information and Intelligence Management

Information and intelligence are important in the Incident Command System (ICS).

Incident management must establish a process for gathering, analyzing, assessing, sharing, and managing incident-related information and intelligence. In NIMS, "intelligence" refers exclusively to threat-related information developed by law enforcement, medical surveillance, and other investigative organizations.

Visual 28: <u>Information and Intelligence</u> <u>Management Discussion</u>

?

What are some examples of sources where you can find and gather information and intelligence?

Visual 29: Unit 2 Summary

You have completed the National Incident Management System (NIMS) Management Characteristics unit.

This unit introduced:

• **Common Terminology** • **Modular Organization** • **Management by Objectives** • **Incident Action Planning** • **Manageable Span of Control** • **Incident Facilities and Locations** • **Comprehensive Resource Management**	• Integrated Communications • Establishment and Transfer of Command • Unified Command • Chain of Command and Unity of Command • Accountability • Dispatch/Deployment • Information and Intelligence Management

Visual 30: <u>Unit 2 Summary Continued</u>

The next unit will provide an overview of the ICS Functional Areas and introduce the roles of the Incident Commander and Command Staff.

Lesson 3: ICS Functional Areas and Command Staff Roles

Visual 1:   <u>Unit 3 Overview</u>

This unit introduces you to the Incident Command System (ICS) Functional Areas and roles of the Incident Commander and Command Staff. By the end of this unit, you should be able to:

- Identify the five major ICS functional areas.
- Describe the role of the Incident Commander.
- Describe the selection of and transfer of command between Incident Commanders.
- Identify the position titles associated with the Command Staff.
- Describe the roles of the Command Staff.
- Differentiate between incident command and incident coordination.

Visual 2:   ICS Functional Areas and Command Staff Roles

Every incident requires that certain functional areas be implemented. The problem must be identified and assessed, a plan to deal with it must be developed and implemented, and the necessary resources must be procured and paid for.

Regardless of the size of the incident, these functional areas are all required.

In case you ever need to assist with an incident, you should understand how the management structure is constructed using the Incident Command System (ICS). This will help you understand your role in the structure and how you may receive information and assignments.

This unit focuses on the five major functional areas and the Command Staff roles. The General Staff roles will be discussed in the next unit.

Visual 3: <u>Five Major ICS Functional Areas</u>

There are five major Incident Command System (ICS) functional areas that are the foundation on which an incident management organization develops.

These functions apply to incidents of all sizes and types, including both planned events and ones that occur without warning.

If you are in an incident and hear these terms, it's important for you to know what they mean. For instance, you may be directed to provide documents to the Planning Section or receipts to the Finance/Administration Section.

Visual 4: <u>ICS Functional Area Descriptions</u>

Incident Command: Sets the incident objectives, strategies, and priorities, and has overall responsibility for the incident.

Operations: Conducts operations to reach the incident objectives. Establishes tactics and directs all operational resources.

Planning: Supports the incident action planning process by tracking resources, collecting/analyzing information, and maintaining documentation.

Logistics: Arranges for resources and needed services to support achievement of the incident objectives (resources can include personnel, equipment, teams, supplies, and facilities).

Finance/Administration: Monitors costs related to the incident. Provides accounting, procurement, time recording, and cost analyses.

Visual 5: Intelligence/Investigations Function in ICS

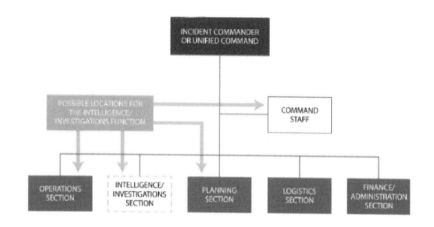

 Note	Intelligence/Investigations (I/I) is a sixth ICS function identified in NIMS. The Intelligence / Investigations function can be established to collect, analyze, and disseminate incident-related information and intelligence for incidents involving intensive intelligence gathering and investigative activity (such as a criminal or terrorist act, or epidemiological, accident or mass fatality investigation).

Visual 6:   Review of Functional Areas (1 of 5)

Which ICS Functional Area supports the incident action planning process by tracking resources, collecting/analyzing information, and maintaining documentation?

Visual 7: <u>Review of Functional Areas (2 of 5)</u>

Which ICS Functional Area sets the incident objectives, strategies, and priorities, and has overall responsibility for the incident?

Visual 8:   <u>Review of Functional Areas (3 of 5)</u>

Which ICS Functional Area conducts operations to reach the incident objectives, establishes tactics, and directs all operational resources?

Visual 9:   <u>Review of Functional Areas (4 of 5)</u>

Which ICS Functional Area monitors costs related to the incident and provides accounting, procurement, time recording, and cost analyses?

Visual 10: <u>Review of Functional Areas (5 of 5)</u>

Which ICS Functional Area arranges for resources and needed services to support achievement of the incident objectives?

Visual 11: <u>ICS Structure</u>

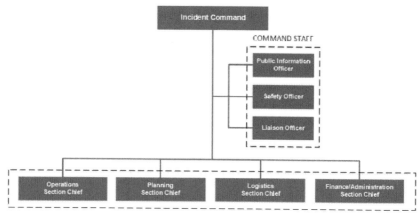

| Note | The standard Incident Command System (ICS) organizational structure is shown here. Incident Command, which could be a single Incident Commander or a Unified Command, will lead the effort and, as needed, assign Command Staff and General Staff. For the remainder of this unit, we will discuss the Incident Command function and the members of the Command Staff.

ICS Organization is Unique

The ICS organization is unique but easy to understand. There is no correlation between the ICS organization and the administrative structure of any single agency or jurisdiction.

For example, someone who serves as a director every day would not normally use that title when deployed under an ICS structure. They would use the ICS title of the position that they were assigned to within the ICS structure. |
|---|---|

This is deliberate, because confusion over different position titles and organizational structures has been a significant stumbling block to effective incident management in the past.

Visual 12: <u>Incident Command Definition</u>

The National Incident Management System (NIMS) defines **command** as the act of directing, ordering, or controlling by virtue of explicit statutory, regulatory, or delegated authority.

When you are using the Incident Command System (ICS) to manage an incident, an **Incident Commander** is assigned. The Incident Commander has the authority to establish objectives, make assignments, and order resources. To achieve these ends, the Incident Commander works closely with staff and technical experts to analyze the situation and consider alternative strategies.

The Incident Commander should have the training, experience, and expertise to serve in this capacity. Qualifications to serve as an Incident Commander should not be based solely on rank, grade, or technical knowledge.

Visual 13: <u>Incident Commander</u>

Let's begin by taking a closer look at the Incident Commander. The Incident Commander is responsible for the overall management of the incident. Overall management includes Command Staff assignments required to support the incident command function. **The Incident Commander is the only position that is always staffed in ICS applications.** On small incidents and events, one person-the Incident Commander-may accomplish all management functions.

Incident Commander

- Command
- Operations
- Planning
- Logistics
- Finance/Administration

Visual 14: <u>Incident Commander Discussion</u>

Why is it critical to establish command from the beginning of an incident?

Visual 15: <u>Incident Commander Responsibilities</u>

In addition to having the overall responsibility for managing the entire incident, the Incident Commander is specifically responsible for:

- Ensuring overall incident safety
- Providing information services to internal and external stakeholders, such as disaster survivors, agency executives, and senior officials
- Establishing and maintaining liaisons with other agencies participating in the incident

The Incident Commander may appoint one or more Deputies. If a Deputy is assigned, he or she should be fully qualified to assume the Incident Commander's position.

Visual 16: <u>Selecting or Changing Incident</u> <u>Commanders</u>

The command function should be clearly established at the beginning of an incident. The jurisdiction or organization with primary responsibility for an incident designates the individual at the scene who is responsible for establishing command and the protocol for transferring command. As an incident becomes more or less complex, command may change to meet the needs of the incident.

When command is transferred, the process should include a briefing that captures all essential information for continuing safe and effective operations.

Note

Reasons for Transfer of Command

There are several possible reasons that command might be transferred. Transfer of command may take place when:

- A more qualified Incident Commander arrives and assumes command.
- A jurisdiction or agency is legally required to take command. For example, the Federal Bureau of Investigation (FBI) is legally required to take the lead for investigations of terrorist incidents.
- The incident changes in complexity. For example, an incident might start in a small area, but spread into the surrounding community, affecting multiple jurisdictions, institutions, or agencies.
- The current Incident Commander needs to rest. On long or extended incidents, there is normally turnover of personnel to accommodate work/rest requirements.

Visual 17: <u>Transfer of Command Discussion</u>

The transfer of command process always includes a thorough transfer of command briefing, which may be oral, written, or a combination of both.

It is also important to remember that the rest of the incident staff should be notified of the transfer of command.

?

What would you include in a transfer of command briefing?

Transfer of Command Process

Note

Transfer of Command Process

The process of moving the responsibility for incident command from one Incident Commander to another is called "transfer of command." It should be recognized that transition of command on an expanding incident is to be expected. It does not reflect on the competency of the current Incident Commander.

There are five important actions in effectively assuming command of an incident in progress.

1. The incoming Incident Commander should, if at all possible, personally perform an assessment of the incident situation with the existing Incident Commander.
2. The incoming Incident Commander must be adequately briefed. This briefing must be by the current Incident Commander, and take place face-to-face if possible. The briefing must cover the following:

   - Incident history (what has happened)
   - Priorities and objectives
   - Current plan
   - Resource assignments
   - Incident organization
   - Resources ordered/needed
   - Facilities established
   - Status of communications
   - Any constraints or limitations
   - Incident potential
   - Delegation of authority

3. After the incident briefing, the incoming Incident Commander should determine an appropriate time for transfer of command.
4. At the appropriate time, notice of a change in incident command should be made to:

   - Agency headquarters.
   - General Staff members (if designated).
   - Command Staff members (if designated).
   - All incident personnel.

5. The incoming Incident Commander may give the previous Incident Commander another assignment on the incident. There are several advantages to this strategy:

   - The initial Incident Commander retains first-hand knowledge at the incident site.

- This strategy allows the initial Incident Commander to observe the progress of the incident and to gain experience.

Visual 18: <u>Deputy Incident Commander</u>

<u>Discussion</u>

?

Scenario: The Deputy Incident Commander will be replacing the current Incident Commander, who needs to attend to a family emergency.

What is the correct action for the Incident Commander?

Visual 19: Delegating Incident Management Responsibilities

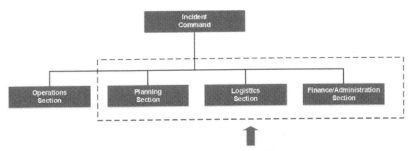

Activated as needed to support the incident response.

The Incident Commander only creates those sections that are needed. If a section is not staffed, the Incident Commander will manage those functions.

Note

The Incident Commander is responsible for all Incident Command System (ICS) functional areas until he or she delegates a function. Since the ICS organization is modular, it has the ability to expand or contract to meet the needs of the incident.

Visual 20: <u>ICS Command Staff</u>

Depending upon the size and type of incident
or event, the Incident Commander may
designate personnel to provide information,
safety, and liaison services. In the Incident
Command System (ICS), the Command Staff
may include:

- **Public Information Officer,** who
  interfaces with the public and media and/or
  with other agencies with incident-related
  information requirements.
- **Safety Officer,** who monitors incident
  operations and advises the Incident
  Commander on all matters relating to
  safety, including the health and safety of
  incident management personnel.
- **Liaison Officer,** who serves as the
  Incident Commander's point of contact for
  representatives of governmental agencies,
  non-governmental organizations (NGOs),
  and private-sector organizations.

Incident Commanders may also choose to
appoint technical specialists (such as legal,
medical, science and technology, or access
and functional needs) to act as command
advisors.

The Command Staff reports directly to the
Incident Commander. In a complex incident,
Assistant Officers may be assigned to each of
the Command Staff functions.

COMMAND STAFF

Visual 21:   Command Staff Overview - Video

Video	***Command Staff Overview Video*** The following video will provide an overview of the Command Staff Officers. Video Duration: 1 minute, 45 seconds

Command Staff Overview

Video Transcript

You've now learned that the Incident Commander has overall authority and responsibility for conducting incident operations. An Incident Commander may assign staff to assist with managing the incident.

The Command Staff consists of the Public Information Officer, Safety Officer, and Liaison Officer, who all report directly to the Incident Commander.

Let's look at the roles of each member of the Command Staff. The Public Information Officer serves as the conduit for information to internal and external stakeholders, including the media and the public.

Accurate information is essential. The Public Information Officer serves as the primary contact for anyone who wants information about the incident and the response to it.

Another member of the Command Staff is the Safety Officer, who monitors conditions and develops measures for assuring the safety of all personnel.

The Safety Officer is responsible for advising the Incident Commander on issues regarding incident safety, conducting risk analyses, and implementing safety measures.

The final member of the Command Staff is the Liaison Officer, who serves as the primary contact for supporting agencies assisting at an incident.

Additionally, the Liaison Officer responds to requests from incident personnel for contacts among the assisting and cooperating agencies, and monitors incident operations in order to identify any current or potential problems between response agencies.

A Command Staff may not be necessary at every incident, but every incident requires that certain management functions be performed. An effective Command Staff frees the Incident Commander to assume a leadership role.

Visual 22: <u>Command Staff Knowledge Check (1 of 3)</u>

?

Which member of the Command Staff is described below?

"I work very closely with Operations to make sure that our people in the field are wearing appropriate protective equipment and implementing safe tactical options."

Visual 23: <u>Command Staff Knowledge Check (2 of 3)</u>

?

Which member of the Command Staff is described below?

"I provide briefings to supporting Agency Representatives and work with them to address their questions and concerns about the operation. I remain visible on the incident scene to all incoming cooperating and assisting agencies."

Visual 24: <u>Command Staff Knowledge Check (3 of 3)</u>

?

Which member of the Command Staff is described below?

"I am the primary contact for anyone who wants details about the incident and our response to it. I serve an external audience through the media and an internal audience including incident staff and agency personnel."

Visual 25:   <u>Command Staff Roles - Activity 3.1</u>

Activity Purpose: To illustrate how ICS can be used to address incident management issues.

Instructions: Working as a team:

1. Review the scenario presented on the next page of your Student Manual.
2. Identify which Command Staff positions would be assigned.
3. Next, if you were the Incident Commander, what specific activities would you delegate to each Command Staff member?
4. Select a spokesperson. Be prepared to present in 10 minutes.

Time: 15 minutes

Scenario:

An unexpected flash flood has struck a small community. As a result:

- Homes, schools, the business district, and the community college are being evacuated.
- Damage to critical infrastructure includes contamination of the water supply, downed power lines, and damaged roads.
- Perimeter control and security in the business district are needed.
- Mutual aid is arriving from several surrounding communities.
- Media representatives are arriving at the scene.

Activity

Command Staff Roles - Activity 3.1

Activity Purpose: To illustrate how ICS can be used to address incident management issues.

Instructions: Working as a team:

1. Review the scenario presented on the next page of your Student Manual.
2. Identify which Command Staff positions would be assigned.
3. Next, if you were the Incident Commander, what specific activities would you delegate to each Command Staff member?
4. Select a spokesperson. Be prepared to present in 10 minutes.

Time: 15 minutes

Scenario:

An unexpected flash flood has struck a small community. As a result:

- Homes, schools, the business district, and the community college are being evacuated.
- Damage to critical infrastructure includes contamination of the water supply, downed power lines, and damaged roads.
- Perimeter control and security in the business district are needed.
- Mutual aid is arriving from several surrounding communities.

- Media representatives are arriving at the scene.

Visual 26: Incident Coordination

Now that we've discussed the Command Staff roles, let's take a look at how the overall incident is coordinated.

Coordination involves the activities that ensure the onsite Incident Command System (ICS) organization receives the information, resources, and support needed to achieve those incident objectives. Coordination takes place in a number of entities and at all levels of government. Examples of coordination activities include:

- Establishing policy based on interactions with agency executives, other agencies, and stakeholders.
- Collecting, analyzing, and disseminating information to support the establishment of shared situational awareness.
- Establishing priorities among incidents.
- Resolving critical resource issues.
- Facilitating logistics support and resource tracking.
- Synchronizing public information messages to ensure that everyone is speaking with one voice.

Visual 27: <u>Command and Coordination</u>

Effective incident management consists of four overarching areas of responsibility:

1. Direct tactical response to save lives, stabilize the incident, and protect property and the environment
2. Incident support through resource acquisition, information gathering, and interagency coordination
3. Policy guidance and senior level decision making
4. Outreach and communication with the media and public to keep them informed about the incident

These objectives are accomplished through the use of the Incident Command System (ICS), Emergency Operations Centers (EOCs), Multi-agency Coordination (MAC) Groups, and the Joint Information System (JIS), respectively.

  Note	The Command and Coordination component of NIMS defines these structures and explains how various elements operating at different levels of incident management interface to achieve the maximum effect through a shared understanding.

Visual 28: <u>Emergency Operations Center Role</u>

Jurisdictions and organizations across the Nation use Emergency Operations Centers (EOCs) as an element of their emergency management programs.

Typically, an Emergency Operations Center (EOC) supports the on-scene response by relieving the Incident Commander of the burden of external coordination and the responsibility for securing additional resources.

An EOC is:

- A physical or virtual location where staff from multiple agencies come together to address imminent threats and hazards
- Staffed with personnel trained for, and authorized to, represent their agency/discipline
- Equipped with mechanisms for communicating with the incident site
- Providing support to the incident by obtaining resources
- Applicable at different levels of government

Note

EOCs may be established at the Federal, state, territorial, tribal, and local levels.

If you are from a non-governmental organization (NGO) or from the private sector, you may be asked to assist at the EOC to assess a situation, provide advice, and make recommendations based on your knowledge and professional expertise.

Visual 29: <u>Joint Information Center</u>

Another coordination entity is the Joint Information Center (JIC). The JIC:

- May be established to coordinate all incident-related public information activities
- Serves as the central point of contact for all news media-when possible, public information officials from all participating agencies should co-locate at the JIC

JICs may be established at various levels of government and at incident sites. Depending on your role in the incident, you may need to direct individuals or organizations to the JIC to obtain information.

Visual 30: <u>Incident Command or Incident</u>

<u>Coordination</u>

?

Do these statements represent Incident Command or Incident Coordination?

1. Establish objectives, make assignments, and order resources.
2. Collect, analyze, and disseminate information.
3. Synchronize public information messages.
4. Establish priorities among incidents.

Visual 31: <u>Unit 3 Summary</u>

This unit introduced you to the:

- Five major Incident Command System (ICS) Functional Areas.
- ICS organizational structure.
- Incident Commander roles and responsibilities.
- Selection and transfer of Incident Commanders.
- Command Staff roles and responsibilities.
- Differences between incident command and incident coordination.

The next unit provides an introduction to the ICS General Staff Roles.

Lesson 4: General Staff Roles

Visual 1:   <u>Lesson 4 Overview</u>

In the previous unit, you learned that the Command Staff supports the Incident Commander who is responsible for overall management of the incident.

This unit introduces you to the General Staff.

By the end of this unit, you should be able to:

- Identify the Incident Command System (ICS) titles used for General Staff members.
- Describe the major activities of the four general staff sections.

Visual 2:   <u>General Staff</u>

To maintain span of control, the Incident Commander may establish any or all of the
following four sections: Operations, Planning, Logistics, and Finance/Administration.

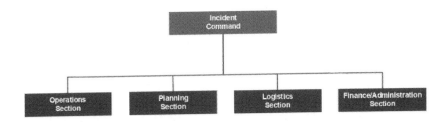

Note	The person in charge of each section is designated as a Section Chief. Section Chiefs have the ability to expand their sections to meet the needs of the situation. As shown here, they report directly to the Incident Commander. Let's take a closer look at these General Staff positions.

Visual 3:   <u>General Staff Overview</u>

In an expanding incident, the Incident Commander first establishes the Operations Section. The remaining sections are established as needed to support the operation.

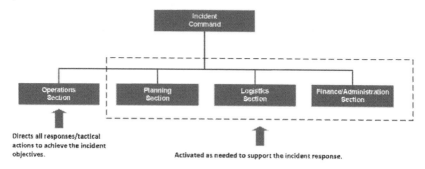

The General Staff overall responsibilities are summarized in the graphic. In an expanding incident, the Incident Command first establishes the Operations Section. The remaining Sections are established as needed to support the operation.

Note

Visual 4:   General Staff Overview Video

Video	**General Staff Overview Video** The following video will provide an overview of the General Staff Sections. Video Duration: 2 minutes, 54 seconds

General Staff Overview

Video Transcript

As you previously learned, an Incident Commander is responsible for all incident management functions including: operations, planning, logistics, and finance and administration.

Depending on the incident needs, the Incident Commander may delegate some or all of these functions by establishing Sections. If a Section Chief is assigned to an incident, he or she will report directly to the Incident Commander.

Together, these Section Chiefs are referred to as the General Staff. Let's take a look at the responsibilities of each Section Chief.

The Operations Section Chief is responsible for developing and implementing strategy and tactics to accomplish the incident objectives. This means that the Operations Section Chief organizes, assigns, and supervises all the tactical or response resources assigned to the incident. Additionally, if a Staging Area is established, the Operations Section Chief would manage it.

The Planning Section Chief oversees the collection, evaluation, and dissemination of operational information related to the incident. It is the Planning Section's responsibility to prepare and disseminate the Incident Action Plan, as well as track the status of all incident resources.

The Planning Section helps ensure responders have accurate information and provides resources such as maps and floor plans.

The Logistics Section is responsible for providing facilities, services, and material support for the incident.

Logistics is critical on more complex incidents. The Logistics Section Chief assists the Incident Commander and Operations Section Chief by providing the resources and services required to support incident activities. During an incident, Logistics is responsible for ensuring the well-being of responders by providing sufficient food, water, and medical services. Logistics is also responsible for arranging communication equipment, computers, transportation, and anything else needed to support the incident.

Another critical function during complex incidents is Finance and Administration. The Finance and Administration Section Chief is responsible for all of the financial and cost analysis aspects of an incident. These include contract negotiation, recording personnel and equipment time, documenting and processing claims for accidents and injuries occurring at the incident, and keeping a running tally of the costs associated with the incident.

We've now introduced you to the four ICS Sections.

It is important to remember that the ICS organizational structure is determined based on the incident objectives and resource requirements. It expands and contracts in a flexible manner. And, only those functions, positions, or sections necessary for a particular incident are filled.

Visual 5:   <u>Operations Section</u>

The Incident Commander determines whether there is a need for an Operations Section and, if so, will designate an Operations Section Chief.

It is up to the Operations Section Chief to activate any additional staffing that is needed. When the Operations Section Chief is designated, the staging and management of operational resources moves from the Incident Command to Operations.

If no Operations Section is established, the Incident Commander will perform all operations functions.

Operations
Section
Chief

Visual 6: <u>Operations Section Major Activities</u>

The major activities of the Operations Section may include:

- Implementing strategies and developing tactics to carry out the incident objectives
- Directing the management of all tactical activities on behalf of the Incident Commander
- Supporting the development of the Incident Action Plan to ensure it accurately reflects current operations
- Organizing, assigning, and supervising the tactical response resources

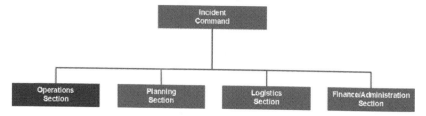

Note	The Operations Section is responsible for directing and coordinating all incident tactical operations.
	The Operations Section:
	• Is typically one of the first organizations to be assigned to the incident.
	• Develops from the bottom up.
	• Has the most incident resources.
	• May have Staging Areas and special organizations.

Visual 7: <u>Planning Section</u>

The Planning Section Chief is designated only
after the Incident Commander determines whether
there is a need for a Planning Section.

It is up to the Planning Section Chief to activate
any additional staffing that is needed.

The Incident Commander will perform all planning
functions if no Planning Section is established.

Planning
Section
Chief

Visual 8: <u>Planning Section: Major Activities</u>

The major activities of the Planning Section may include:

- Preparing and documenting Incident Action Plans
- Managing information and maintaining situational awareness for the incident
- Tracking resources assigned to the incident
- Maintaining incident documentation
- Developing plans for demobilization

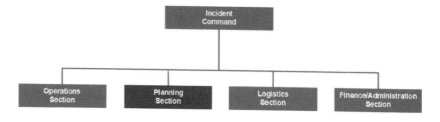

Visual 9: <u>Logistics Section</u>

The Logistics Section Chief is designated only after the Incident Commander determines whether there is a need for a Logistics Section.

It is up to the Logistics Section Chief to activate any additional staffing that is needed.

The Incident Commander will perform all logistics functions if no Logistics Section is established.

Logistics
Section
Chief

Visual 10:   <u>Logistics Section: Major Activities</u>

The Logistics Section is responsible for all services and support needs, including:

- Ordering, obtaining, maintaining, and accounting for essential personnel, equipment, and supplies
- Providing communication planning and resources
- Setting up food services for responders
- Setting up and maintaining incident facilities
- Providing support transportation
- Providing medical services to incident personnel

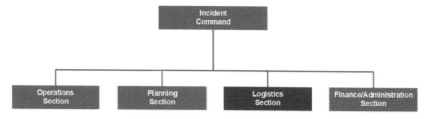

Visual 11: <u>Finance/Administration Section</u>

The Incident Commander determines whether there is a need for a Finance/Administration Section at the incident.

If so, the Incident Commander will designate an individual to fill the position of the Finance/Administration Section Chief.

The Time, Compensation/Claims, Cost, and Procurement Units may be established within this section.

Finance/Administration Section Chief

Visual 12:   Finance/Administration Section: Major Activities

The Finance/Administration Section is set up for any incident that requires incident-specific financial management. The Finance/Administration Section is responsible for:

- Contract negotiation and monitoring
- Timekeeping
- Cost analysis
- Compensation for injury or damage to property
- Documentation for reimbursement (e.g., under mutual aid agreements and assistance agreements)

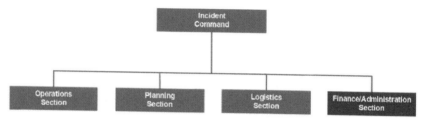

Visual 13: <u>Section Chiefs Activity 4.1</u>

Activity

Section Chiefs Activity 4.1

Activity Purpose: To review the General Staff Section responsibilities.

Instructions: Working individually:

1. Review the table in your Student Manual.
2. Identify the correct Section Chief for each statement.
3. Be prepared to share your answers in 5 minutes.

Time: 10 minutes

	Statement	Which Section Chief?
1.	In advance of severe flooding, there is a need to get generators and communications equipment to the Staging Areas to equip advance response teams. My Section is responsible for making sure the needed equipment arrives at the Staging Areas.	
2.	As the response is underway, my Section tracks all personnel participating in the response.	
3.	My Section conducts response activities such as search and rescue, and first aid services being provided to disaster survivors.	
4.	I support the incident response activities by overseeing contracting for needed supplies and	

	Statement	Which Section Chief?
	services that are not already available.	

Visual 14: <u>General Staff Review (1 of 5)</u>

?

Which member of the General Staff is described below?

"In advance of severe flooding, there is a need to get generators and communications equipment to the Staging Areas to equip advance response teams. It's my responsibility to make sure the needed equipment arrives at the Staging Areas."

Visual 15: <u>General Staff Review (2 of 5)</u>

?

Which member of the General Staff is described below?

"As the response is underway, my section tracks all personnel participating in the response."

Visual 16: <u>General Staff Review (3 of 5)</u>

Which member of the General Staff is described below?

"My section conducts response activities such as search and rescue, and coordinates medical services being provided to disaster survivors."

Visual 17: <u>General Staff Review (4 of 5)</u>

?

Which member of the General Staff is described below?

"I support the incident response activities by overseeing contracting for needed supplies and services that are not already available."

Visual 18: <u>General Staff Review (5 of 5)</u>

?

Which member of the General Staff is described below?

"Throughout the incident and during the after-action review process, the reports that we develop will be very useful."

Visual 19: <u>General Staff Functions - Activity 4.2</u>

Activity Purpose: To reinforce participants' understanding of General Staff functions.

Instructions:

1. Working in groups, review the scenario presented in your Student Manual.
2. Use what you have learned to answer the questions for each part of the activity before proceeding to the next page. Write your answers on chart paper.
3. When you have answered each set of questions, move on to the next page.
4. Select a spokesperson and be prepared to discuss your answers to all the questions in 15 minutes.

Time: 20 minutes

Scenario Part 1: A store employee at a small shopping mall discovers a package leaking a noxious smelling chemical in a storage room. No one is sure how long the box has been there, or how long it has been leaking. Employees and customers are beginning to complain about feeling lightheaded and nauseous. The business owner calls 911. In the meantime, the mall security manager arrives to see why people are rushing out of the store. The security manager establishes the initial ICS organization.

 Activity	**General Staff Functions - Activity 4.2 Part 1** Activity Purpose: To reinforce participants' understanding of General Staff functions. Instructions: 1. Working in groups, review the scenario presented in your Student Manual. 2. Use what you've learned to answer the questions for each part of the activity before proceeding to the next page. Write your answers on chart paper. 3. When you've answered each set of questions, move on to the next page. 4. Select a spokesperson and be prepared to discuss your answers to all the questions in 15 minutes. Time: 20 minutes Scenario Part 1: A store employee at a small shopping mall discovers a package leaking a noxious smelling chemical in a storage room. No one is sure how long the box has been there, or how long it has been leaking. Employees and customers are beginning to complain about feeling lightheaded and nauseous. The business owner calls 911. In the meantime, the mall security manager arrives to see why people are rushing out of the store. The security manager establishes the initial ICS organization. Question:

- In the ICS organization described above, the mall security manager has assumed which role?

Visual 20: <u>General Staff Functions - Activity 4.2</u> <u>Part 2</u>

Scenario Part 2: A Battalion Chief and hazmat team arrive at the scene. In addition, a law enforcement patrol car with one officer has arrived to help with perimeter control.

General Staff Functions - Activity 4.2 Part 2

Scenario Part 2: A Battalion Chief and hazmat team arrive at the scene. In addition, a law enforcement patrol car with one officer has arrived to help with perimeter control.

Question:

- What must happen before the HazMat Battalion Chief assumes the Incident Commander role?

Activity

Visual 21: <u>General Staff Functions - Activity 4.2</u>

Part 3

Scenario Part 3: To maintain span of control as the incident expands, the Incident Commander establishes an Operations Section.

General Staff Functions - Activity 4.2 Part 3

Scenario Part 3: To maintain span of control as the incident expands, the Incident Commander establishes an Operations Section.

Questions:

- What is the role of the Operations Section?

Activity

- What is the ICS title of the person in charge of the Operations Section?

Visual 22: <u>General Staff Functions - Activity 4.2</u> <u>Part 4</u>

Scenario Part 4: After the first hour, the Incident Commander establishes a second Section that will develop the Incident Action Plan and track the status of resources on the scene.

General Staff Functions - Activity 4.2 Part 4

Scenario Part 4: After the first hour, the Incident Commander establishes a second Section that will develop the Incident Action Plan and track the status of resources on the scene.

Question:

- What is the correct title of this Section?

Activity

Visual 23: General Staff Functions - Activity 4.2

Part 5

Scenario Part 5: In an interview, the business owner mentions that she has received threats from a recently terminated employee. The substance has yet to be identified. Given these circumstances, there is a need to find witnesses and locate people who may have come in contact with the package. Interview areas have been set up in the mall parking lot. There are an increasing number of response personnel at the scene, creating the need for communications support along with food and drinks.

General Staff Functions - Activity 4.2 Part 5

Scenario Part 5: In an interview, the business owner mentions that she has received threats from a recently terminated employee. The substance has yet to be identified. Given these circumstances, there is a need to find witnesses and locate people who may have come in contact with the package. Interview areas have been set up in the mall parking lot. There are an increasing number of response personnel at the scene, creating the need for communications support along with food and drinks.

Activity

Question:

- Which Section is responsible for providing these support resources?

Visual 24: General Staff Functions - Activity 4.2 Part 6

Scenario Part 6: Cleanup is complete, and the few exposed customers and staff have been located and are undergoing treatment. The operation is now shifting to an ongoing investigation of the disgruntled former employee.

General Staff Functions - Activity 4.2 Part 6

Scenario Part 6: Cleanup is complete, and the few exposed customers and staff have been located and are undergoing treatment. The operation is now shifting to an ongoing investigation of the disgruntled former employee.

Question:

Activity

- Which resources would you demobilize?

Visual 25: <u>Unit 4 Summary</u>

This unit introduced you to:

- The Incident Command System (ICS) roles of the General Staff.
- The major activities of the four ICS General Staff sections.

The next unit focuses on how the ICS applies to you and your agency or organization.

Lesson 5: How ICS Applies to You

Visual 1: <u>Unit 5 Overview</u>

In this unit, you will be given an opportunity to apply information presented in the previous units.

You will be given a scenario involving flooding and you will be asked to select which NIMS Management Characteristics are demonstrated throughout the scenario.

By the end of this unit, you should be able to:

- Identify how the National Incident Management System (NIMS) Management Characteristics apply in specific roles.
- Identify how the National Incident Management System (NIMS) Management Characteristics apply in specific situations.

Visual 2:   Emerald City Flood Scenario

Activity Purpose: To reinforce participants' understanding of NIMS Management Characteristics.

Instructions:

1. Working in groups, review the scenario presented in your Student Manual.
2. Use what you have learned in the course to answer the questions. Write your answers on chart paper.
3. Select a spokesperson and be prepared to discuss your answers to the questions.

Time: 10 minutes

Scenario: It has been raining heavily for the past seven days in Emerald City. The Emerald City and Liberty County Emergency Management offices are preparing for a response to a possible flood situation. Residents are starting to ask questions about the rising river and lake levels, and are wondering if they will need to leave their homes.

Management Characteristics-Knowledge Check/Scenario Questions

Note

NIMS Management Characteristics

A *NIMS Management Characteristics Summary* is provided at the end of Unit 2 (Instructor Guide and Student Manual) for assistance in completing the knowledge checks.

Activity 5.1

1. You are an American Red Cross Disaster Program Specialist in charge of teams trained to help in sheltering displaced persons. You have been notified by your office to be prepared to deploy to conduct shelter operations. Your supervisor has asked you to come to the office to begin organizing volunteers and get prepared to set up shelters, if tasked.

What NIMS Management Characteristic are you supporting?

Activity

2. You are a Geographic Information System (GIS) specialist who normally works at the Public Works Planning office. You are directed to report to the Emergency Operations Center (EOC) and have been assigned to the Planning Section Chief. You will be producing maps to display potential flooding impacts in the city and county.

What NIMS Management Characteristics are you supporting? Discuss all that may apply.

Visual 3:   Emerald City Flood Scenario: Update 1

Instructions:

1. Working in groups, review the scenario presented in your Student Manual.
2. Use what you have learned in the course to answer the questions. Write your answers on chart paper.
3. Select a spokesperson and be prepared to discuss your answers to the questions.

Time: 10 minutes

Scenario Update 1:

Raining has continued for three more days and the flooding is expected to reach its highest point today. The flooding has caused residents to evacuate their homes in anticipation of rising floodwaters. Basement flooding to the first-floor level is anticipated.

The local Nursing Home is assessing the situation to determine if an evacuation of residents is necessary.

Visual 4:   Emerald City Flood Scenario: Update 1 (Continued)

The Liaison Officer, with the support of the Public Information Officer, is in contact with business owners to determine if any of their stored chemicals will be affected by the flooding, causing possible contamination downstream.

Based upon previous floods, it is a high priority to establish shelters for evacuees early on. The Emergency Operation Plan pre-identified the following shelters: Lawrence College Auditorium and Lafayette Middle School.

Due to the complexity of the incident, the Incident Commander has expanded the Operations Section to include an Evacuation Group. The Evacuation Group Supervisor immediately contacts the Lawrence College President and the Lafayette Middle School Principal to begin the process of establishing shelters in those facilities.

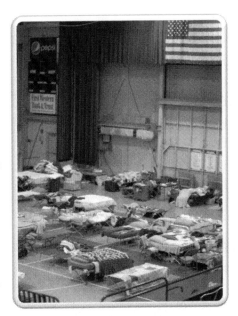

Management Characteristic-Knowledge Check/Scenario Questions Update 1

Activity 5.1: Scenario Update 1 Questions

1. You are the American Red Cross liaison in the Emergency Operation Center and you print up a list of the location of materials necessary to outfit the shelters. Materials stored in both facilities are adequate to meet the initial needs. Both the College and the Middle School are implementing their respective plans and are establishing necessary staffing to support the shelter requirements.

What NIMS Management Characteristic is being demonstrated?

Activity

2. Due to the complexity of the incident, the Incident Commander has expanded the Operations Section to include an Evacuation Group.

What NIMS Management Characteristic is being demonstrated?

3. You are the City Fire Chief and are evaluating the supervisory structure needed to manage the Incident Command Post staff. You also request senior representatives from the Health Care community and from Public Works to help develop objectives to protect the residents of the nursing home and the critical water resources of the community.

What NIMS Management Characteristics are you supporting? Discuss all that apply.

Visual 5:   Emerald City Flood Scenario: Update 2

Instructions:

1. Working in groups, review the scenario presented in your Student Manual.
2. Use what you have learned in the course to answer the questions. Write your answers on chart paper.
3. Select a spokesperson and be prepared to discuss your answers to the questions.

Time: 10 minutes

Scenario Update 2:

The Evacuation Group is reporting that homeowners are beginning to move their families out of the area. The American Red Cross has opened two shelters, one at the Lawrence College Auditorium and one at the Lafayette Middle School.

Visual 6:   Emerald City Flood Scenario: Update 2 (Continued)

The Nursing Home is attempting to move 55 patients from their skilled nursing care facility and is asking for assistance from Emergency Medical Services, the Fire Department, and the School Bus Company.

Acme Chemical is reporting first-floor flooding of their chemical processing plant. They are not reporting any chemical release but are closely monitoring their facility.

Calls are coming into the Emergency Operations Center from concerned citizens wondering about the safety of the municipal drinking water. Additional concerns about the wellbeing of water fowl and fish in the river and lake are being voiced because tourism, fishing, and hunting are a major part of the economy in the area.

Additional resources are needed for evacuation, sheltering, sandbagging, water level and chemical monitoring, traffic control, and scene security at other Incident Command Posts. Several media helicopters have arrived in the area to film the ongoing operations.

Management Characteristics-Knowledge Check/Scenario Questions Update 2

Activity 5.1 Scenario Update 2 Questions

Instructions:

1. Working in groups, review the scenario presented in your Student Manual.
2. Use what you've learned in the course to answer the questions. Write your answers on chart paper.
3. Select a spokesperson and be prepared to discuss your answers to the questions.

Time: 10 minutes

1. General Staff immediately come together and begin developing strategies. General Staff Chiefs are:

- Evaluating the supervisory structure needed to manage the Incident Command Post staff
- Identifying resource shortfalls
- Updating planning documents.

What NIMS Management Characteristics are you supporting? Discuss all that apply.

Activity

2. You are the Operations Section Chief at the Incident Command Post and request that all response communications be conducted using a pre-determined set of frequencies. You also remind everyone in the field to use plain language.

What NIMS Management Characteristics are being demonstrated? Discuss all that apply.

3. The Operations Section has determined that the Emergency Medical Services, the Fire Department, and the School Bus Company will be assigned to the evacuation of the Nursing Home. They will all converge at City Hall and will be dispatched, as appropriate, to begin

---

the rapid and safe movement of the residents to their temporary shelter locations.

What NIMS Management Characteristic is being demonstrated?

Visual 7:   <u>Emerald City Flood Scenario: Update</u> <u>3</u>

The nursing home's emergency plan calls for relocating residents with acute medical care needs to the Community Hospital. Residents without acute medical needs will be sheltered.

The American Red Cross, in collaboration with the Salvation Army, are managing the shelters and providing food for displaced residents.

The Public Works Department and the Health Department are monitoring the water intake at the Water Treatment Plant for signs of chemical contamination. Public Works crews are placing sandbags to protect the Water Treatment Plant.

Management Characteristics-Knowledge Check/Scenario Questions Update 3

Activity 5.1 Scenario Update 3 Questions

Instructions:

1. Working in groups, review the scenario presented in your Student Manual.
2. Use what you've learned in the course to answer the questions. Write your answers on chart paper.
3. Select a spokesperson and be prepared to discuss your answers to the questions.

Time: 10 minutes

1. You are the President of Lawrence College. You and the American Red Cross Shelter Manager have contacted the Incident Command Post concerning the ability to meet the nutritional and long term pharmaceutical needs of the elderly residents. The Liaison Officer requests assistance from the Emergency Operations Center.

Activity

What NIMS Management Characteristic is being demonstrated?

2. You are the Middle School Principal. You and the Shelter Manager notify the Incident Command Post that several people are complaining of severe stomach cramps, diarrhea, and vomiting. You ask for assistance from medical and public health personnel. You also request additional sanitation supplies, bedding, and bathing materials. The Operations Section Chief is requesting additional assistance from the Emergency Operations Center for a specialized monitoring team to be deployed to the shelter to survey for a possible outbreak. Survey results will be shared with Health and Public Works departments.

What NIMS Management Characteristic are you supporting? Discuss all that apply.

Visual 8: Emerald City Flood Scenario: Update 4

The river levels have steadily receded and residential property owners are anxious and attempting to return to their properties. Public Utility Crews are assisting City Building Inspection crews in the inspection of evacuated homes for safety and structural integrity before allowing residents to move back in. Drinking water qualities are being monitored and cleanup and damage assessment activities are beginning.

The American Red Cross and Salvation Army report that most evacuees have found longer-term temporary housing. Very few evacuees remain in their shelters, and shelters are anticipated to be closing soon.

Emerald City Health Department personnel, along with representatives from the County and the State Health Departments, are monitoring the water intakes and the city drinking water for any signs of contamination. Nothing significant has been detected so far. The County Health Department is also monitoring private wells as requested by the landowners.

Visual 9:   Emerald City Flood Scenario: Update 4 (Continued)

The Nursing Home reports that water has receded from their building and that they are beginning cleanup procedures. They expect to finish their cleanup, including mandatory inspections by the State Health Department, within a week.

Because the activities are shifting from response to recovery, the mayor of Emerald City has asked the Incident Commander to prepare to demobilize and transfer command of the incident to a Unified Command consisting of Emergency Management, the Emerald City Health Department, and the Emerald City Department of Public Works.

The newly formed Unified Command will focus on restoring essential services, providing a safe re-entry for displaced residents, and completing a thorough damage assessment. The transfer of command will take place at the end of the next operational period.

Management Characteristics-Knowledge Check/Scenario Questions Update 4

Activity 5.1 Scenario Update 4 Questions

Instructions:

1. Working in groups, review the scenario presented in your Student Manual.
2. Use what you've learned in the course to answer the questions. Write your answers on chart paper.
3. Select a spokesperson and be prepared to discuss your answers to the questions.

Time: 10 minutes

1. As phasedown of shelter operations has begun, the American Red Cross Disaster Operations Supervisor has directed you to begin re-assigning shelter staff personnel and releasing those that are no longer required. You direct released staff to checkout.

What NIMS Management Characteristic are you supporting? Discuss all that apply.

Activity

2. You are the Middle School Principal. As shelter operations are beginning to phase down, you continue to be concerned about the illness suffered by the residents of your facility, which was confirmed to be a food borne illness from donated food. Since school will resume soon, you want to reassure school staff and parents that there are no residual risks. You request the newly formed Unified Command for a public information broadcast and a representative from the Health Department to share information regarding the illness and be available to answer questions.

What NIMS Management Characteristic is being demonstrated?

Visual 10: <u>Unit 5 Summary</u>

You have now completed Unit 5.

In this unit you have:

- Identified how the National Incident Management System (NIMS) Management Characteristics apply in specific roles
- Identified how the National Incident Management System (NIMS) Management Characteristics apply in specific situations

Visual 11: <u>Course Summary</u>

You have now completed this course.

You should now be able to:

- Explain the principles and basic structure of the Incident Command System (ICS).
- Describe the NIMS Management Characteristics that are the foundation of ICS.
- Describe the ICS functional areas and the roles of the Incident Commander and Command Staff.
- Describe the General Staff roles within ICS.
- Identify how NIMS management characteristics apply to ICS for a variety of roles and discipline areas.

Visual 12: <u>IS-100.c Final Exam Instructions</u>

When the review is completed, follow these Final Exam instructions:

1. Take a few moments to review your Student Manual and identify any questions.
2. Make sure that you get all of your questions answered prior to beginning the final test.
3. When taking the test online …

- Go to http://training.fema.gov/IS/crslist.asp and click on the link for IS-0100.c.
- Click on "Take Final Exam."
- Read each item carefully.
- Check your work before submitting your answers.

Visual 13: <u>Certificate of Completion</u>

To receive a certificate of completion, you must take the multiple-choice Final Exam and score at least 75 percent on the test.

Upon successful completion of the Final Exam, you will receive an e-mail message with a link to your electronic certification.

Visual 14: <u>Course Evaluation</u>

Completing the course evaluation form is important. Your comments will be used to evaluate the effectiveness of this course and make changes for future versions.

Please use the course evaluation forms provided by the organization sponsoring the course.

Made in the USA
Las Vegas, NV
14 December 2024

14178500R10090